To: Hazel
I hope
my poetry
inspire you
to explore
your dreams!

The Art of

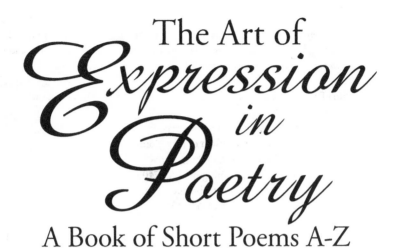

Expression in Poetry

A Book of Short Poems A-Z

JACQUELINE ZANDERS

BALBOA.PRESS

A DIVISION OF HAY HOUSE

Balboa Press books may be ordered through booksellers or by contacting:

Balboa Press
A Division of Hay House
1663 Liberty Drive
Bloomington, IN 47403
www.balboapress.com
844-682-1282

Because of the dynamic nature of the Internet, any web addresses or links contained in this book may have changed since publication and may no longer be valid. The views expressed in this work are solely those of the author and do not necessarily reflect the views of the publisher, and the publisher hereby disclaims any responsibility for them.

The author of this book does not dispense medical advice or prescribe the use of any technique as a form of treatment for physical, emotional, or medical problems without the advice of a physician, either directly or indirectly. The intent of the author is only to offer information of a general nature to help you in your quest for emotional and spiritual well-being. In the event you use any of the information in this book for yourself, which is your constitutional right, the author and the publisher assume no responsibility for your actions.

Any people depicted in stock imagery provided by Getty Images are models, and such images are being used for illustrative purposes only. Certain stock imagery © Getty Images.

Print information available on the last page.

ISBN: 978-1-9822-6638-7 (sc)
ISBN: 978-1-9822-6640-0 (hc)
ISBN: 978-1-9822-6639-4 (e)

Library of Congress Control Number: 2021906905

Balboa Press rev. date: 04/27/2021

This book is dedicated to my parents,
Jack and Alnedia Zanders.
I miss them both dearly, and I wish they
were here with me to share this moment.

Jack and Alnedia

The first time I met you was on September 3rd.
You held me in your arms tightly, and you never let me go.
You caressed me and told me that you loved me,
And then you took me home.
You provided nurture and protection,
Which often came with correction.
You invested in my development,
As you taught me to be independent.
You instructed me to pray,
Each and every day,
And that is why I'm here today.
Jack and Alnedia, mommy and daddy,
My love for you will never fade away.

Acknowledgments

Thank you to the following individuals who, without their contributions and support, this book would not have been written:

I want to thank my brother, Keith Zanders, for his support and for always encouraging me to pursue my dreams.

I want to thank my aunts Dorothy Young and Gwendolyn Johnson for their maternal guidance and prayers during this journey.

I want to thank my uncle Joe McHomes and my friends Deborah Thompson, Fonda Kelly, Lucita Broussard, and Tanya Dunbar-Stone for persuading me to write my book.

Lastly, I want to thank all my family and friends for their prayers and inspiration.

Introduction

Jacqueline

I never knew I had the propensity
To express my reflections in poesy.
I stumbled upon it serendipitously.
Now it's a source of tranquility.
It allows me to express my creativity
In a way that offers me serenity.
I pursue my endeavor to be a poet with sincerity.
I want my thoughts and words to impact humanity.

Contents

Preface XV

❖ Letter A
   1.   All or Nothing 1
   2.   And Why Did You Enter Matrimony? 2
   3.   Anger Management 3
❖ Letter B
   4.   Be Free... 7
   5.   Beware of Lust 8
❖ Letter C
   6.   Confidence 11
❖ Letter D
   7.   Destiny.. 15
❖ Letter E
   8.   Everlasting Love 19
❖ Letter F
   9.   Forgiveness 23
   10. Friendship 24
❖ Letter G
   11. Girl, You're Complete 27
❖ Letter H
   12. Happy and Single.. 31
❖ Letter I
   13. "I Love You" 35
❖ Letter J
   14. The Jovial Giant 39
   15. Just Stop It 40

❖ Letter K

    16. Keep Striving 43

❖ Letter L

    17. Let Go 47

    18. Living in the Moment 48

    19. Look to the Sky 49

    20. Love Divided 50

    21. Love That Jazz 51

❖ Letter M

    22. Maximize Your Potential 55

    23. Message to My Sisters 56

❖ Letter N

    24. Never Again 59

❖ Letter O

    25. Opposition (Critics) 63

❖ Letter P

    26. The Past Is the Past 67

    27. Patience 68

    28. Pillow Talk 69

    29. The Potter and the Clay 70

    30. Proceed with Peace 71

❖ Letter Q

    31. Queen 75

❖ Letter R

    32. Respect 79

    33. Reunion 80

    34. Roller Coaster 81

❖ Letter S

    35. Silence Is a Beautiful Thing 85

    36. Still a Woman 86

❖ Letter T

    37. Tenacity 89

    38. Tender Kiss 90

    39. True Beauty 91

❖ Letter U

    40. Unconditional Love...................................... 95

    41. Unexpected Shift.. 96

❖ Letter V

    42. Vibes 99

❖ Letter W

    43. Wake Up 103

    44. What Lies Beneath...................................... 104

    45. What Love Is.. 105

    46. What People Say 106

    47. Whatever!... 107

    48. Why...?..108

    49. Will We Ever Get There? 109

❖ Letter X

    50. X-Ray Vision 113

❖ Letter Y

    51. You've Got This.. 117

    52. Your Version of Me 118

❖ Letter Z

    53. Zen 121

About the Author 123

Preface

The Art of Expression in Poetry: A Book of Short Poems, A–Z is a compilation of fifty-three poems derived from experiences and knowledge obtained during my life. The poetry discusses a wide range of topics and issues that we encounter throughout life and a few **love** stories. I hope my insights provide inspiration, motivation, and courage, as well as humor.

A

All or Nothing

It has nothing to do with the competition.
If he wants you, he will show you attention.
Stop making yourself look desperate
To win his affection by any effort.
You are a queen, and you should expect to be treated as such.
Settling for less
Will leave you without much.
Respect yourself, and don't give in to his whims
For temporary comfort and moments that fill you to the brim.
Availability to you should not be readily accessible.
Let him know that you are not disposable.
Demand more
If you want to explore.
If not,
Lead him to the door.

And Why Did You Enter Matrimony?

If you have an aversion to being loyal and faithful,
Why did you bow your knee to make an appeal with the jewel
To form a union that you are not inclined to honor
By being unfaithful with every encounter?
You knew you were incapable of monogamy before the vows,
So why did you agree to be a spouse?
Was it because of the tax break,
Or did you want your image on top of a wedding cake?
Why did you enter matrimony
Only to continue to do your folly and to cause acrimony?
Remove yourself from the sanctity of marriage.
Stay clear to diminish the drama and damage.

Anger Management

I refuse to change who I'm going to be
Based on your treatment of me.
I'm going to remain the same,
Even when you try to inflict pain.
I will deny you the power to change my output,
And the way I approach life with a positive outlook.
You have the right to speak your mind;
However, it's full of poison and words that are unkind.
I choose to limit my interaction with you
Because it appears,
You're short of a clue.
On that account,
In order to keep my sanity
And secure my healthy mentality,
I will love you from afar in my chamber
As a method to manage my anger.

B

Be Free

Be free to love with a generous heart.
Be free to love till it never departs.
Be free to embrace life with tenacity.
Be free to know who you are and to live relentlessly.
Don't hesitate; just orchestrate,
And let your life illuminate.
Be free to live your life.

Beware of Lust

Sometimes we think we are in love,
But it could be a strong case of lust.
In lust, we find ourselves wanting to be consumed by the flame,
Night and day, regardless of the strain.
When we're in lust, we are void of a clear perspective;
We are only thinking about the next encounter.
But the explosives from the encounter can lead to disaster.
Proceed with caution if you're in lust
To avoid getting burned by your own burning obsession.
I've been there before.
That's why I can say, "Beware of lust."

C

Confidence

Confidence is a trait that is necessary to attain your goal.
The absence of it will make you lose focus and be fearful.
You have what it takes to execute and be successful.
Doubting yourself will result in delay and keep you off schedule.
Believe in your competency to produce and be bountiful.
Release all apprehension and be masterful.
Embrace your greatness to be sensational.

D

Destiny

The light is always leading you to a place of destiny.
Keep negative energy and distractions at bay
To avoid hindering your view to your pathway.
Have clarity at hand each and every day
To steer you in the right direction along the way.
However, in the event of drama and disarray,
Know that you can adjust your route and get underway.

E

Everlasting Love

How precious is love
That is sent from above.
It runs deep as the ocean
And is perpetually in motion.
It never surrenders,
And it remains very tender.
It endures through the years
And many shed tears.
No matter how many seconds pass,
This love will surely last.

F

Forgiveness

We have amnesia when it comes to our
shortcomings and mistakes.
Yet, we have a photographic memory of others'
defects and don't give them a break.
In this life, you will have the opportunity to cause havoc.
You're not immune to situations that create panic.
When you find others in a quandary,
Don't take it upon yourself to disperse their dirty laundry.
One day you will find yourself in a predicament
that's the opposite of pleasant.
Surely you would appreciate forgiveness
from others minus the judgment.
No one is perfect.
I'm sure we all agree.
Therefore,
Let's be merciful to the highest degree.

Friendship

True friendship takes time to cultivate.
Use wisdom as you navigate.
Build trust along the way.
Establish boundaries to obey.
Give as much as you take.
Be quick to apologize when you make a mistake.
Lend support during hardships.
Demonstrate how you value the relationship.
Celebrate victories and opportunities to advance.
Love unconditionally, no matter the circumstance.

G

Girl, You're Complete

You don't need a man to define you;
You're complete.
You don't need his income to obtain financial freedom;
You're complete.
You don't need his approval to be exceptional;
You're complete.
You don't need his guidance to pursue excellence;
You're complete.
You don't need his connections to strive for perfection;
You're complete.
There is a difference between wanting and needing a man.
That is a fact you truly, must understand.
You're whole, and you're grand,
And don't need a man to stand.
You're complete.

H

Happy and Single

The state of singleness is not a curse.
Some may say; it's the reverse.
You have the liberty to come and go sans converse.
The income is yours to disburse.
Decisions you make remain enforced,
No one to tell you to change your course.
You can live spontaneously and go on a quest,
And live the life that suits you best.
Nothing against wedded bliss and for better or worse,
Nonetheless,
Everyone is not yearning to be married in the universe.

1

"I Love You"

How many times have I said, "I love you"?
But was it always true?
Was it triggered by impulse and my desire to have a **boo**?
Jumping in deep without having a clue
Of who you really are and if this is something I should pursue.
But in haste
I gave you my heart,
Which was wrong from the very start.
There was never any evidence on the chart
To validate my decision to impart
Feelings that were doomed to depart.
Can't blame you for my mistake or distraught;
It was my choice to give love devoid of thought.

The Jovial Giant

The jovial man who stood as a giant to many,
Not because of his stature or that he was mighty.
He was a giant because he had so much to impart.
He had a generous heart from the very start,
Continuously sharing his love and affection
With no motives or deception.
He withheld judgment during difficult times.
He only offered words of encouragement to help me climb.
His devotion wasn't exclusive to me.
Many experienced his dedication to the highest degree.
He was constantly ready to assist
And voluntarily commit,
When he believed there was a mission
That required his attention.
Although his natural presence isn't here,
His spiritual essence remains to instruct us to persevere.

Just Stop It

Stop stressing and having anxiety,
Trying to keep up with the Joneses in society.
Stop the fighting and the rivalry,
Competing to see who gains the most commodity.
Stop the insults and vulgarity
As a means to communicate your disharmony.
Stop judging others' morality
In efforts to deflect your hypocrisy.
Stop acts of hatred in humanity
To validate your sense of supremacy.
Stop it all today!
Embrace our diversity
To gain stability,
To live in a world of liberty.

K

Keep Striving

Life is full of disappointments.
Do not allow the setbacks to keep you from striving.
Be diligent and resilient,
As you strive to realize your dreams.
And when you see the fruits of your labor,
Then you will know that you've achieved your goals.
Keep moving and rejoicing,
Because you will triumph through any storm.

L

Let Go

The past was yesterday.
Disallow negative vibes to overstay.
Discard things and people that produce decay.
Don't let the baggage of your past hide like a stowaway,
Lurking in secret and causing dismay,
Making you feel like you're a castaway.
Release it now to void a replay.
Shun recycling the chaos and the melee.
Begin a new journey right away.
Create an unblurred routeway.
Stay focused on the present and make headway
To a future full of hope and brighter days.

Living in the Moment

Moments are precious; you must seize the day.
Make the most of whatever you have in your possession today.
Find pleasure in your current status.
Don't postpone happiness and become callous.
At this moment, your life may not resemble all that you desired.
Nevertheless, take satisfaction in what you have acquired.
Enjoy your life at every point in time,
Then you will experience contentment for a lifetime.

Look to the Sky

When I look to the sky,
I see beyond the natural eye.
I perceive the possibility to achieve
And accomplish whatever I believe.
There is nothing to restrict my ability to reach for the stars
And limit my capacity to advance and go far.
My potential is defined by me and what I exemplify,
So I look to the sky to aim high.

Love Divided

How can love survive

If our convictions are divided?

I believe in God we trust.

When I say that, you look at me with disgust.

You're free to declare your disbelief,

Yet

When I express my belief, there is grief.

Currently, we are at an impasse.

Who knows if this love will last?

There's no room for compromise;

That statement must be emphasized.

I will not deny my faith

As a remedy to avoid scathe.

Our connection is endless, and my love runs deep for you.

Even so, I can't choose you over what I believe is true.

Maybe someday we will have the same point of view.

At that time, our love can be renewed.

Love That Jazz

Melodies filling my head
Rhythms flowing widespread
Vibing to the beat, that's so sweet;
It makes me want to get on my feet.
That **Jazz** is so smooth and so cool.
Love it like it's a precious jewel.

M

Maximize Your Potential

Maximize your potential
By eliminating nonessentials.
Steer your vigor toward the beneficial,
And minimize the inconsequential.
Engage in the fundamental
To avoid the detrimental.
Stay methodical,
And give preferential
To actions that are prudential
To be exceptional.

Message to My Sisters

Beauty comes in all shapes and sizes.
It doesn't matter your ethnicity.
We are all beautiful.
We are the rainbow on the earth.
God made us beautiful.
We are all royalty.
The essence of beauty.

N

Never Again

Prince Charming is your name.
Howbeit,
It's only a farce in the game that you play.
You approached me with gifts and charm to seduce me like prey.
You had no intentions to develop and cultivate
a relationship that would last.
Your objective was to fulfill your appetite and to have a blast.
It took me a minute to see past the charade.
The knowledge gained revealed the masquerade.
Although it was hurtful and produced disdain,
I learned my lesson, and it will never happen again.

O

Opposition (Critics)

My life is my life; don't tell me how to live it.
This is my life, and I don't need consent.
You discuss my life and criticize my decisions,
Questioning if I have a clear vision.
But your vantage point requires revision,
Because we are on different missions
And also,
You are blinded by your ignorance.
We all have different paths for our lives to follow.
We must choose the path that will not lead to sorrow.
So instead of judging each other,
Just live your life and respect each other.
My life is my life,
And I will live it my way.

P

The Past Is the Past

Living your life stuck in the past.
Pushing the pause button on life because of bitter memories,
Holding off on living your best life due to agony.
But the past is the past.
Live for today and far from yesterday.
Unshackle the anguish.
If you hold on to pain
It will make you insane.
Don't let your history
Make you stand still in misery.
Don't let the past keep you crying.
Release it now and start living.
Arise with strength today, and let your heart
Lead you to a fresh start.
Because the past is the past.

Patience

There's a time for everything.
Don't give up.
Sometimes we approach life with a designated time
For the plans of our lives to materialize.
And if there is a hindrance,
We allow disbelief to reside
And the opinion of naysayers to rise.
Never let anyone make you feel like you've been denied.
Some aspirations take a while.
And when it's attained, you will have a smile.
Always remember,
There's a time for everything.
Don't give up.

Pillow Talk

I love the moments of pillow talk.
When we come together,
At the end of the day.
We rest our bodies as we lay.
You look into my eyes,
And I look into yours too.
We share current events
And highlights of the day.
We talk about our achievements
And what we have to pay.
We have deep discussions
On politics and such,
With transparency,
Listening carefully.
We never debate.
We purely escape,
Sharing the pleasure of intimacy.
That pillow talk,
So rich and so sweet,
And that affectionate discourse
Would sometimes lead to other things.
So I must go now
And enjoy my pillow talk.

The Potter and the Clay

The pain was from the pressure that was
applied during the molding process.
You were shaping me into the woman you designed me to be.
The carving removed the layers that were obstructing my vision.
You chiseled the remnant and sculpted me
according to the purpose of my life.
Now I can go forth and execute the plan you created just for me.

Proceed with Peace

Peace is a concept that is essential.
Deficiency in it is not beneficial.
Create a mindset that facilitates calmness.
When adversities occur, persevere with stillness.
Collect your thoughts to be strategic.
Dismiss all pessimism and rhetoric.
Proceed with composure and poise,
And evict the agitation and the noise.

Q

Queen

I may not reign over a monarchy
Or have an aristocracy in my pedigree,
Nevertheless,
I am a queen, and I know my identity.
I expect to be treated and respected with gentility.
I will not accept behavior that is contrary.
And anything less is not satisfactory.
Know your worth and your nobility.
Expect royal treatment and live gracefully.

R

Respect

Why do you approach me with no dignity?
No, I'm not your "Shawty."
Dude, I'm over forty.
Don't yell at me and get feisty
If I don't respond to you nicely.
Do we have a history?
Your name isn't listed in my directory.
That being the case,
What makes you think I must acknowledge you directly?
The lack of connective ties explains my austerity.
Nothing against you, but you're not a crony,
And you shouldn't expect me to react with affinity.
Please respect my liberty
If I choose not to reply to your "flattery."
I appreciate it sincerely.

Reunion

The way you caressed my hand as we rode in the car
Made me feel like we were never apart.
Our reunion did not take place for thirty-seven years.
That fact alone
Brings me to tears.
If I would have stayed, instead of run away,
We would have more memories to display.
Now I can only imagine what would have been
If I hadn't jumped ship but explored the feelings I had within.
I know we can't relive the past.
For this reason,
I have no regrets to broadcast.
I am thankful for the hours we shared.
What happens next
Is up in the air.

Roller Coaster

At first glance, it was instant chemistry.
Despite that, we didn't immediately explore our sensory.
Whenever our orbits crossed, there was
a recurrent sense of gravity.
The unexpected meetings were moments of ecstasy.
And then suddenly, we chose to take the leap.
We plunged into the passion and went in deep.
Then before we knew it, the excitement started to seep,
Which led to chapters of constant grief.
Our expectations differed tremendously.
As a consequence, we didn't arrive to a state of consistency.
We went back and forth with no success;
To be perfectly honest, we didn't give it our best.
Even though the love we shared was very intense,
It didn't flourish because solidarity was absent.

S

Silence Is a Beautiful Thing

Why must you habitually insert your opinion voluntarily?
All information shared with you doesn't
require your commentary.
Wait for an invite to express your opinion.
Your viewpoint is not a mandatory requirement to make a decision.
Stop injecting your stance and feelings
In family's and friends' ways of living.
Keep the peace by speaking the least.
Avoid becoming an antagonist.
Demonstrate your devotion.
Exclude expressing your notion.
If an invite to assert is extended,
Then your slant will be permitted.

Still a Woman

Do not minimize my worth
If I have not given birth.
My womb does not define me as a woman,
And my ability to nurture is not based on conception.
My value is based on my impact in my world
And my character traits that have been modeled.
I will not allow anyone to label me as barren.
With seeds of knowledge and love, I cultivate people to fruition.
I know I am honored and respected by my tribe.
All other opinions,
Will not affect my vibe.

T

Tenacity

When you tackle life with purpose,
You see your design flourish.
Navigating the trek that keeps you focused
On your quest to succeed and finish.
Conquering the challenges on your course,
Never surrendering to the anguish.
Steadily galvanizing ideas that reinforce
Your tenacity to prevail and accomplish.

Tender Kiss

I didn't know I wanted you again until I felt
your tender kiss touch my lips.
The kiss was gentle but intense.
I never experienced that type of kiss from you.
Now my mind wonders,
Is this the new you?
And should I explore the tender kiss to see if there's more?
In the past, we have not always seen eye to eye.
This kiss was something that caught me by surprise.
Could it be our time apart has softened your heart?
Maybe it's not a coincidence that our paths have crossed again.
Perhaps the tender kiss was a prelude to
a destiny waiting to give birth.

True Beauty

Is beauty what we see,
Or does it reside in the unseen?
We praise the exterior
And disregard the interior.
We focus on the visual
Instead of the individual.
The presence of beauty is not certified by the visible.
True beauty is authenticated and endures in the invisible.

Unconditional Love

We trundle through life trying to find that perfect love.
But we must realize that in this life,
There is no perfect love.
When we let go and love with no restrictions,
It's unconditional love.
I'm not perfect, and you're not perfect.
But together, we're pure perfection.
I threw out my list, and you threw out your list.
Now together, it's pure bliss.
I had my doubts, and you had your doubts.
But together, we stuck it out.
I had my limits, and you had your limits.
Now together, we're limitless.
It's unconditional love.

Unexpected Shift

Have you ever experienced an abrupt change
When there was no pause to prepare or rearrange?
Suddenly your mindset required adjustment to maintain
Strong resilience and a stable domain.
You didn't anticipate the event to occur.
Now you must accept and endure.
This shift is filled with uncertainty.
You must embrace it with assurance and valiancy.
Summon strength and courage
To eliminate fear and establish a firm passage.
Never doubt your wherewithal to subdue
What is presented to you,
Even when it comes out of the blue.
You are equipped to manage the predicaments in life,
As well as the obstacles that may cause strife.
Persevere through the adversity
To display your audacity.

V

Vibes

What is your vibe?
Do you exude positive energy in moments of catastrophe?
Are you a negative voice in occasions of rejoice?
Do you still have the same demeanor
when others become meaner?
Does your mood fluctuate if you can't
get your plans to generate?
Do you hold a grudge when your love refuses to budge?
Is it your goal to take hold in efforts to obtain control?
Do people feel your jollity instead of your anxiety?
Are you hopeful for the future regardless
of the level of pressure?
Your vibe defines you.

W

Wake Up

Hey,
I feel like I got something to say.
I think that the world is in disarray.
Politicians fighting but not finding a way
To solve the issues of life we face every day.
Is this the image they want to portray?
Are they people who are just in it for pay?
Is this what it feels like to be betrayed,
All the promises made thrown away?
Is this how the game is played?
"Forget what I said yesterday";
This can't be the message they want to convey.
Stop the madness without delay!
Change the course of action today.
Allow unity, wisdom, and love to be on display.

What Lies Beneath

What lies we tell to portray the image of success.
Despite the fact that you have done your best,
You still feel the need to embellish and impress.
Distorting the facts of your journey and quest,
Changing the narrative you want to express.
Reshaping your history and what you profess,
Omitting the segments that caused much distress.
Appearing as if you never regress
And had challenges that made you digress.
Admission of hardship does not minimize your progress.
It shows your determination and finesse
To continue to fight, no matter the test.
Be authentic with the story you confess.
Because transparency is a trait
We all should possess.

What Love Is

Does he call you instead of sending a text?
Does he make sure your needs are addressed?
Does he share his possessions without request?
Does he take care of you when you need to rest?
Does he support your dream until it manifests?
Does he protect you like he was wearing a superhero's vest?
Does he shield you from circumstances
that may keep you stressed?
Does he spend time with your family free of protest?
Does he look at you like you leave him breathless?
Does he express his devotion to you with truthfulness?
That's what love is at its best.
And if you experience that, then you are truly blessed.

What People Say

Does it really matter what people say?
Are they with you to help you face the
dilemmas of life every day?
Are they paying your bills at the end of the day?
Are they comforting you when loved ones go away?
Are they offering refuge if you need to break away?
Are they extending support if family members go astray?
Are they responding when you send out a mayday?
Will they be with you when your hair turns gray?
If the answer is no to all the above,
Then why should you care what people say?

Whatever!

Never let anyone's opinion
Reshape your mission.
Ignite your ambition,
And stick to your decision
To pursue your vision.
Your dream is not in their possession,
Thus, they have no comprehension.
Who cares about the opposition.
You don't require permission,
To explore your great commission.
Don't let the clique alter your position
And affect how you implement with precision.
They don't understand your determination,
Or your resolution to chase, whatever the condition.
Even if there are episodes of tribulation,
That often lead to complication,
Do not allow the commotion
To keep you from reaching the culmination.

Why...?

Why do you waste time and energy on things that have no value?
Why do you allow erroneous advice to take
you down the wrong avenue?
Why do you criticize and slander people you've never met?
Why do you live beyond your means and get into debt?
Why do you receive gifts, though are hesitant to give?
Why do you hold animosity that is very destructive?
Why do you always assume the worse before
having the chance to converse?
Why do you demand loyalty, but in return, extend the reverse?
Is it because you have lost your way
And allow foolishness and lack of foresight to overlay?
It may be prudent to terminate this method of operation.
Dissolving it will reduce the discord and the agitation.

Will We Ever Get There?

Will we ever get there,
When we're all treated fair?
How long will it take for that day to come?
It's my prayer that day will be soon.
Will we ever get there,
When they see you but not your hue?
Will we ever get there,
To a place where we're all free from fear?
How long will it take for the "Dream" to be true?
Simply open your heart and change your point of view.
How long will it take?
Will we ever get there?

X

X-Ray Vision

My perception is clear.
The powers that be will not keep me in fear
With all the nonsense they produce to bring people to tears,
Constantly fighting year after year.
But is this a ruse to keep us from discovering the truth
About all the decisions that are made in the booth.
Avoid getting distracted by all the drama.
Stay informed to lessen the trauma.
Which is caused by a lack of knowledge and data
And not being aware of issues that matter.
Develop keenness.
Maintain awareness.

Y

You've Got This

There is no singular method to process the events of life;
You must do what suits you right.
Following others may lead you to plight,
And eventually, you will lose your form and fight.
Be true to yourself, and conquer all with might.

Your Version of Me

With a quick glance,
You made your assessment
With no knowledge of my investment.
You have no cognizance of the sacrifices I've made
Or the damages I've paid.
You judge me with no clue
Of all the hell I went through
To get to this place of peace and confidence,
While also
Erasing the need for approval and acceptance.
So,
I've come to the conclusion
That it's just your illusion.
With that said,
I have no yen or necessity
To persuade you to think differently.

Z

Zen

Find that delightful place of serenity.
Detoxify your mind of thoughts that cause perplexity.
Indulge in activities that produce tranquility.
Remove anything that will generate irascibility.
Release all anxiety.
Dismiss the negativity.
Concentrate on the positivity.
Create an atmosphere of placidity.
Implement behavior that will induce equability.
Remain peaceful to sustain this state of stability.

About the Author

Jacqueline Zanders is a Long Island, New York native who currently resides in Atlanta, Georgia. In addition to writing poetry, she is an aspiring songwriter and life coach. When not writing, she enjoys listening to music—especially jazz—interior designing and fashion consulting.

CPSIA information can be obtained
at www.ICGtesting.com
Printed in the USA
BVHW042011060722
641299BV00015B/542